Noise from the Laundry

Noise from the Laundry

Weyman Chan

Talonbooks

Talonbooks
P.O. Box 2076, Vancouver, British Columbia, Canada V6B 3S3
www.talonbooks.com

Typeset in Adobe Garamond and printed and bound in Canada.
Printed on 10% post-consumer recycled acid-free paper.

First Printing, Second Editon: 2009

The publisher gratefully acknowledges the financial support of the Canada Council
for the Arts; the Government of Canada through the Book Publishing Industry
Development Program; and the Province of British Columbia through the British
Columbia Arts Council and the Book Publishing Tax Credit for our publishing ac-
tivities.

LIBRARY AND ARCHIVES CANADA CATALOGUING IN PUBLICATION

Chan, Weyman
     Noise from the laundry / Weyman Chan.— 2nd ed.

Poems.
ISBN 978-0-88922-626-5

     I. Title.

PS8555.H39246N63 2009   C811'.6   C2009-901807-1

Contents

1.

say what, Wey

I'm cooking chilli and enjoying life

shawl

War:
the fighting fish are plumes in their bowls.
I'm no better than
a mouth
harangued
and habit-formed;
they commit me to memory
then watch my fin dissolve.

So the sea held its breath
once for me
and the dew drop of my mother's passing
held the spine
of its elder snowflake;

a disturbed
and broken colour
came in at low angle.
Her shaft could not've
snuffed
a wiser sage
turned to one side
exhaling ink in my
slow stroke
without derision.

one billion love

What news from the far-off colonies?

The eunuch admiral Zheng He sends his emissary from the middle kingdom.

What are his demands.

There are no demands.

Are we not wary? He has spies of course.

No your majesty. Gifts, not spies. Saffron, ginger, tea, jade, pearls, silk.

What are his intentions?

Pride, your majesty. Ballsy, oolong pride.

I pay him, this tour guide who's a student at Beijing university. It's August, 1989. 2 months after Tiananmen. We walk the stones along Shanghai's Bund. Freighters and ships, slow passage, scurfing rumour about the sweeping up of remains to hide the true number of bodies killed and torched in the square of that one-mind system. Meanwhile, a cook shuffles past us balancing 2 baskets on a shoulder pole: a brown hunk of moose nose, and a black bear's paw. Over the coo of such delicate meats, a red-luck couple will be joined in marriage dipped in one billion love. He showed me that the Chinese word for "writing" is the "bird" character, nestled under the "house" symbol.

Birdhouse equals hostage; after that stroke ends, bird cuts through mouth and ear hole. A flick in the pan
spawns the white sea,
        thleh-doo meaning, "writing words"
          thleh-sui meaning, "spilled water"
    sounds like—sounds like—

Mr. Curda signalling the launch of my rocket. Cow pies in a cow field just outside Calgary. My North Star runners slick with shit. I was partnered with Manfred, whose uncle taught him that there was no holocaust. His sleek black rocket with three silver tailfins went *cheuuuuuuuuuup*, ate up the blue. How could someone so wrong be so free?

Manfred's wordless grin: my rocket went the highest.

I squatted in the thick, held my breath.
My rocket scooped the air
                                        so high
it wrote the second coming   then spiralled
down down down
and broke open
the pale blue egg.

cherry blossoms at night

Yoshino cherry blossoms. Fallen
and prized above all others in Noh.
They fall at night and the Emperor does not know
what wind takes the ceramic balloon bombs across
a town in Manchuria. The Emperor
doesn't know bubonic fleas can blossom in a bomb.
That same year, 1939,
in the wet riceless fields west of Hoi Seng,
my father's ankles have swollen a second time
from starvation. The third time you die.
He's catching a few carp and frogs for dinner.
Swamp reeds ripple through his fever—
yesterday he sold his youngest brother and still
the Japanese are coming.
He hears hem-flutter
and sees a flying goddess, with her moonbeam raiment
draped across her shoulders, descending
upon a pond that lifts its mirror
up to her bright butter skin.
She sheds her glitter on a willow bush.
Settles into water-folds.
Dad advances, takes her shining scarf.
It parts and swallows
his wrist in higher waters,
threatening to pull him up
to the celestial world.
But he refuses to go, and the fabric dims.
She must now crawl before his heart.
When she bears him a boy
that resembles his little brother,
her fate is sealed. She will never fly off.
Cloud-ladders will storm the moon gates for her;
heaven won't rest without her.

She will be a conduit
for the designs of birth and death,
will appropriate blossoms
that sinter the night air with
so much more.

goodbye to the foster parents

On the last day, there is a war
over the tying of laces.
"He knows how to tie them himself, Mr. Chan," says Katie.
I'd pooped in my day clothes,
walked around in my shit all day singing.
Now Dad's come for me and my sister,
to build up his cloud immortal soup recipe,
spin that salesman-alchemy of his before leaving.
In his pocket is a photo of our new mother.
And White Rabbit toffees shweet shlow shweet.
Uncle Phil has two horses and not enough hours
in the day for giving us one last ride.
We're as dumbfounded as this foster home on an Airdrie farm.
Dad gets to lift me up to the saddle.
His holding me is the same as Uncle Phil's—
blanket-comforting safety. But
who is he I'm taught he's my Dad but tiny feet and bud-fingers
don't know where to hold. Talk slow to God when you pray,
Auntie Mary once said, her bedpost whispers drawn in.
Go ahead then. Outgrow the stripes
of your pajamas and be your own charge—
autumn pulls both ways,
while the dark waits like a hungry fish to jump through.
We are all orphans
because God is. He's the romantic one at the harp of things,
tisk-tisking our kowtows at Mom's grave,
checking his watch, pulling crud
from his ponytail—
They don't pray to a personal deity, but they can sure throw a mean dice,
God thinks to himself;
then adds, *die. Throw a mean die.*

Same anxiety when the dragon waited
to devour whatever son the moon-woman
gave birth to. Religion

13

plugged my roof gutter. I had to push out
its dense colostomy of leaf-rot,
and then I heard God, falling from the drain spout.
He was filthy, red-eyed, smelly, hopped up on the season's vari-hued elm,
carrying an assortment of duffle bags and
a guitar case whose emblem read, Remember Me.
It was also on an autumn day
after the horse ride
and after the won ton soup and moo goo gai pan,
that the one father turned away
towards his stable and his pitchfork,
while the other took me shlow shweet shlow
far from the hill of slain leaves
just before the lights went out
among army beetles, scaffold swans
and sock rot willow. I,
who used to be an emperor among
dairy cows,
stood at the doorway
of my own crib.

he who tells stories in his old age

" … there's human hair in soya sauce from China. They blend it in to enhance the
colour."

what's trying to come through? what medicine
through the ears can be poured by projector where
retirement from the service calls us inside
the everbright sitting temple
serving tea to fallen immortals and soft-slippered earth spirits?

this Chinese   always a lesson within lessons

beginning with orphan pie faces cute to touch and picked up by the dozen

the toy blue piano passed between crib bars when me and my sister
owned the space without MaMa or BaBa
enchanted fingers in our mouths   our touch each note on the toy
blue piano keys
where the notes know you are only a child
filling the brightening day

in deep middle age   I'll tell my children something
you can live through anything
because the desperation that
never called itself desperation
made you listen with clear sails and wait with open arms
while laughter overtook
those sad long eyelids.

zzzzodiac birthday

You think that once every 12 years you've returned.
That someone more intimate than a mirror
knows how you listen for pain in
sweet voices and wait
at kiosks where bright light sharpens its arrows.

The fastest sense is sight, but you've failed
to widen. Potala bridge into thin air. In the bell of their sleep,
beaded prayer and estrus-robes.
        The red shore listens.
Belly-first, the monks disappear.
Feng shui already knows
what it is you seek. So I must go on feeding budgies.
Rita must continue dripping red candle wax
on pavement to protest Tiananmen.
Fabricate the public. Collectivize the existential.
You are discrete but solicitous and compliant.
Say you are on holy ground—
bamboo thicket-cloud
following the loess-soaked river.
Anonymity, birds, ash. Don't worry. You will still
be hunted down and maimed ...

see Lenin in his cell holding a quill carved from a matchstick
dipped in an inkpot made of dried bread.

                        When the guard came
the story goes, he swallowed match and inkpot whole—the year
of the rabbit also ruled him in parables.

a slower sunrise

Again I'll listen
to the morning. Perish,
hair-pulled koan

speaking on behalf of the bathed and the pure

every light pretends to part with truth
on the cloud's fiction
the world's yarn. Blushed
pink to luck   sadness
swinging in the background. It all reminds me
of staying. Some days are like that

plumped anvils perched on blue
and hurt seeps in
like forgiveness.

The day that bore its own beginning
before the storm
now shines me to my skin and burns
in a good way. Why? Look
at clouds
at life. It's what
the silver lining needs.

queen elizabeth

Not just the school's long passivity
but her place in it. While the bees of
late summer throw their stripes to sugar and light,
the day feels lapped and lived over
in passing. Amazement's first decree:
ecru eyeliner, tall teenaged resistance
warrior. My daughter's only small, her armour
wears the fall of night
emptying old rabbits
on beggar's berber and favourite monkey bar swings.
What old playthings will resurrect.
Although I insisted that nothing would be new
on this first day,
my daughter forgets me, grows into the hands
of waiting doors.

2.

wait on tables

shimmy?   *Shine?*

delicate atrocities

It was on this year's anniversary of Hiroshima
when usefulness and playfulness dovetailed.

The radio voice switched gears
to enlighten me about the Rotterdam Toe-sucker—

a confidence man, a wave of heat
that left no musk or sandal-print. The usual woman

asleep in her striped cabana tent
would turn over and dream

a rhythmic dream, toes dipped in sun-lifting splash.
While the man's mouth screwed her piggies

and swallowed her sand,
she would not wake up, or chose not to—

maybe she was seduced, felled,
eroded in the hourglass

by such stark devotion
kneeling before her, avid,

taking permission, not asking for it. In Dutch,
I found out, the word for permission is *toestemming*.

children of the corn

If, Mabel, life and events could be stretched along one axis,
north would be purity, and south would be complication.

Therefore, Mabel, go north.

                     For too long, these hooks
called family these transfusions called daily grind
have coursed through like iodine
when all you needed was blood from the Iroquois elders who found you again
       and brought you back to their fields,
       youngest of Three Sisters—

suicidal, yet found.   We were in your car
in '87, the beginning

vase full of baby flesh, strips of baby flesh you
          (were forced to)   eat

                 and later you saw eyes
faces of dead babies   stuffed into burlap sacs
their foreheads blending with potato bulges
                 go ahead   *tell*
               no one
             will believe you

,couldn't be spoken of in those weird gatherings of terror among the variegated
maple pastoral. Like a scene out of *Children of the Corn.*

I believe you
I've loved you too many years
       to deny you that house full of pain so let's go Mabel.
Let's go let's go let's forget this road radio lullaby going down slow. Let's go to the sky bear
who plays at the north star.

You always said your most powerful dream
brought down the Bear Spirit
who crouched among your cares for this world
and counted your strength
as her own.

if Kafka were a ballroom dancer

Shovels scraping, my daughters fill spring snow in the wheelbarrow.
They are making yard soup.
Cotoneaster slurry, mud, more dead poplar leaves,
fierce mixing, air weeds bind with charms
particular to *pow pow*, my youngest daughter's make-believe language
that can conjure anything:
influenced by their dear Auntie Yvonne, Bird Lady,
her studio of herons, canvas hummingbirds of perpetual spring.
I intimated that her favourite colour must be red,
so sparingly daubed in this field
of disrepair, you'd have to get up early in the morning just to
pin each drop judiciously
on lives otherwise overcast
and liable. I have been
put here for—(name a reason).
If my kids had longer fingers, they might pluck from the sky
ladybugs, then make a game of it,
reaching out to include shore birds, arctic
terns, their limbs fanatic as Japanese crabs
diving in for the feast and then my job might be
to weigh the pros and cons
of fairy tale, how wonderment failed Kafka's father even then.
I've been that father, often distancing
myself from them. And maybe
in their underwater travels without me,
my beautiful daughters will find the sea cave
of the Pearl Bearer. They'll pry her ancient vault open,
only to be swallowed by an oyster, evil yet misunderstood,
having devoured its own pearl ages ago
to become the dream-searcher unfulfilled,
sentencing those
who would in turn become ageless.

In their desire for home, there could only be one option:
my daughters must come back as rare gems,

worn by a sorcerer
until good undoes him, and only then
would my pearls-as-girls find their way home to me.
Now I see the pattern.
This brown grass combed by ice,
rabbit scat in the upper blades,
sets the stage for our reunion.
As more leaves gather at the shore of the drain spout, far away
from the world's predators, my daughters' laughter
seems to lack a certain spell.
If it weren't for their boil and bubble,
I would have forgotten
how I got here.

for Uncle Dong Fei who just keeps going

Uncle Dong Fei is 104, fragile in winter. He has it
standing still, those shakes in his
bleached red-gnarled, soaked-to-the-bone son of a
laundryman's hands—
a committed Christian whose YMCA-sponsored wife
back in 1920 was the talk of Chinatown—
and I ask him how old he is, really,
and he just laughs, waters the African violets
in his room and lets me feed him congee with
oong-goo and *mook-ngee.*
My father brings him
a plastic cream cheese container, full of tofu jello,
home-made *au-foo fa.* "*Mm heck-uk*, can't eat so much,"
Uncle Dong Fei protests,
waving those thickened calluses and bleached nails.
He still starches his own collars, irons and presses
his 6 shirts and 4 pants on visiting days
when we can watch him. His eyes brighten
when the nurse brings in the iron and ironing board.

Look, listen, and learn, my father seems to indicate, by
the way he leans forward. Uncle Dong Fei
takes a giant gulp of peppermint water
and spews the finest mist cloud from his lips.
A rainbow leaps up and leaves its arc.
He begins ironing as the droplets
fall on his sleeve, his chest pockets,
the detail
around each cuff button. His early shakes are
stilled and purposeful, the hot iron's prow glides over a white sea,
looking for refuge, unwrinkling vastness
as it goes along,
and his ship never stops curving in spite of itself,
and I think of rescue within rescue
because there must be a point to this, and
Uncle Dong Fei,
Uncle Dong Fei who just keeps going.

"despite the cold laser rejuvenation,
her support group is strong"

pipa   lute

er-hu string loosed

cherrr-yooohhhyai-eehuuuii.

Sad   so oystery
T'ang silk spoken by *Li*, 30th hexagram, crushed
virgin, little lightnings breaking wind,
doomed either wanting "to die or get the hell outta there"

vermillion daughter
slow scudding boundfoot-falls
wedded in absence of
arrow through her 9 elixirs
logo ribbon fridge magnet

cherrr-yooohhhyai-eehuuuii

sad   so symphony-Altaic
consort Mongolese,
her upper lip *wan wu*
Ten Thousand Emanations bathe
in cinnabar. *Kun:* pure yin

skin lixiviates *aqua fortis.*
Bathe to draw out fever and confession then
            perfume   thy noose

you and I
for Jaspreet Singh

The indifferent
sets

a higher order in which
we aren't citizens. If
the reproduction of
sound must upstream
the mind from
monument to moment, then
      hearing
      is the
      will.
Axon syntax pause.

History

stems
from the quantum fray
and time

through music   divides
time past
and light. The sender
without a message.

The taut logic between noise
and meaning is indefinable
but key. To go without
saying is the default setting

that says everything.
Thought, intent, purpose.
One voice
stays inside another, which stays

inside yet another.
Every day we enact
the blameless voice or
the voice of certainty.
And as we listen
for an answer,
the world leans a little
closer.

rock. paper. scent. whatever.
for Ashok Mathur

"I composed a poem and showed it to no one,"
Lady of *The Gossamer Years* writes in her diary eleven hundred years ago.
Deep melancholy
attends her invitations to Iris Festivals and Sumo Banquets,
years waiting for her husband,
the imperial secretary, to come home.
He writes to her rudely,
"I have been told that when one goes off to the mountains,
people sometimes write to him."

I crunch down on the warmth of my chocolate croissant,
slice my tongue across its velvet
and the moon-behind-the-shoji-screen's whisper. Pardon
the sticky mouth and fingers—but a poem
about lost face should not skimp on comfort.

Looking out from this pier of the Blue Parrot Café,
cicadas, temple bells and petal-dusted pines
seem close enough to the sentiment
expressed by the cellphone diva behind me
shouting to her boyfriend across the water
to direct his high-powered binoculars at her.
He's only a dot—one of several small dots—
crossing a high-rise condo balcony
in the distance. Granville Islanders
enjoy eating while being seen, and
wherever propriety leads, the courtesan or her love letters must follow.
But who rides asleep and ferries swollen rivers
to deliver these doves of sentiment?

The Lady knows the price of words mixed with tears—
they alone span the intrepid overcast
promise of being set apart, linked by marriage
to one master, true to his turning autumn leaves.

Rain, approaching hooves, all things,
listen for her discrete betrayal.

Behind her, ahead of me, gulls and cormorants dive at nothing,
or maybe they see hidden crumbs between crests,
vague intimations
grailing the deep. Birds don't like to admit
any finality beyond flight itself.

From robed layers turned inward,
to riddled phrases of a thousand long years,
there has to be the smallest
pit of truth, the one
frail thing she and I hold on to,
because it is hopeful, unsent, and folded
in the wide sleeve behind our backs.

under the lilac tree he hums

Narrowing is joining; divot pressed
to pivot-fold the bamboo leaf around.
A clay spoon to scoop the raw white drops
of hard, glutinous rice. Cup the left hand. Place
a sliver of red lye wood. Or, fill instead
with mung beans, finger length of pork sausage,
dried shrimp and yolk. Top off
with another spoonful of rice, then close the bundle
with one more leaf. Bind with new or used cotton twine
and slap the contents to even out the four corners.

This is how *doong* are made. Their simplicity
saves explaining the voice down in his chest
when it hurts most to be spoken.
Instead, he boils the *doong* for at least four hours
in a metal drum
and when we least expect it, he serves them warm.

towards

Noise through a sleepy window
will change a chair into something more present
than love.

Wake of lightning this tender
red shifts its note
from brazen to abstract.

Nietzsche once said, stars shouldn't
be held over you. Look at how they climb down from the rising past,
needy and flute folded
like an opening towards happiness.

Stars and us together,
a wide break in the trees,
will let the distance come inside.

3.

and whether or not

they've come as animals fallen from the sky

always

1.

an inkline
unwinding under hell

bandied sword to cannon eats chariot
the king hemmed in both sides
checkmate

van Gogh yellow emulates the sower
field with Dad and his water buffalo
if they could be poured
my need to know

The sage-king from his temple-wilderness
strikes the chime-stones leading osprey and phoenix, sabre-toothed
and common tigers alike, to the outward shape
her art inside her mouth
perineal snow dunes
outline our concentric listening—
the spirits of the dead and demons innermost,
then peoples of the eight directions,
then the beasts and insects. Assembled thus,
the sages teach all and leave none out.

Seven a.m. I am face-to-face with the crazy guy
perched high and satisfied on the bicycle inside his head.
He pins his forearm under my syringe.
To him I explain lithium levels only because

his deep Sufi eyes ask
for no pain. I loosen
the tourniquet   he takes my arm
shows me his window
points up at a star and says, I named that one for you.

2.

Outside these walls called Palace Love
forgetting has become an engagement—
a pretty cloud shifts her hair
from swallowtail to hag switch.
The sword horizon's stuck in rust and
no one to raise the karst
on what was once mine by right.
Look, this mill is a tired waterclock perched over the mirror-stream
when once I held
her majesty. Eunuchs combed my hair then,
and washed gently on me
what had in turn been taken from them.

Retreat downriver. During war you have
daughters, not sons, said Tu Fu. With daughters
you can wed your way to peace.

Night rides a black horse over Calgary. Fallujah sits its cold cement step for
the little ones who watch a tiny bright star. It winks to shrapnel
from its toy edge.
Run to capture fireflies with mongol sleeves—stun them.
Then make a lantern out of your fingers.
What do glow bugs know of prison balconies, palace walls?
This is the T'ang gossip column—
road silk on shadow,
the secretarial still-life a kind of
girl-in-pool meets flute music,
and the teachers are always whispering behind mental screens.

I was inside a poem about winter grass.
Beneath a rabbit's footprint-thaw
broke waters of laughter, and bamboo, and flies—
how can that be? the hours ask—

spitting dissolves ghosts, which is why they fear us.
One might say that if the sun is subsistence then
the moon is poetry, wary of its own deftness
                    and I would think that being dragged in
by a late rabbit was the way to refinement until I realized, hey,
that rabbit was me, tumbling across the wide chora,
the tourists' abyss, *Rugosa* rose by any other name,
pearled veils that extrovert fur, flat earth drumhead spanned
heuristic, star, shooting star, make a wish—mine.

She did not look immortal. Her claws were not dirty from elixir-grinding.

I studied this furred burrower rising up on her mantid legs.

Sympathy in those stand-still eyes, paws that dig powerfully,
her corollary of headspace much like
a proverb that acts alone,
while everyone suspends itself.

Rabbit washes often to offset death,
whiskers quick to overwrite smell with smell,
said the trenchcoat nurse.

On a Wednesday morning in August of 1986,
I forgot who I was. There was a sallow farmer,
someone whose lungs were elsewhere, high up in the trees, drying.
I had to take his blood. I wrapped the tourniquet
and stuck the needle into his thick, rope-rolling arm vein.
The vein cracked audibly, torn sausage skin.
When crimson black blood spat into the tube, I travelled through
        to my own heart.
I was blessed and married on an airplane, ageless in her arms,
the harp's pelvis played my daughters home and

the man, I found out, couldn't move. He was motionless
in the last slights of astrocytoma. Eyes glanced
off the hospice walls
belching out line code, star-shaped cells mudding
the brain, beautiful name, astro-sights
and sounds tell me
crickets in the cistern, cowbells on the edge of a million cows
wishing for their mothers who've touched you
before the five a.m. milking, will bend and graze
over those days halved then quartered, minutes, seconds—

     Rabbit turned down the tunnel. She led me
with her deep deep thump   I felt her dark
thumb around my eyes I felt
the heartbeat's titrations through fenestrations
in Bowman's Capsule, down the tubes and out—then she said to me,

Wear this

What I said, unable to see

Wear this game

What game I asked

Wear this game that never satisfies

and she with her snuffed out white fur and combed-back fascicles,
her sing-for-your-own-death alibi, released me from this tunnel.

3.

What did she mean?
Wear the robes of his drunkenness,
like when Li Po drowned reaching for
the moon's surface on felled water, so close
he could touch the eternal bunny, moist fur that
rippled black and overturned?
What did she mean?
My sleep was flaked, scudded.

The sages teach all, and leave none out.

And if the moon is poetry,
changing rollercoasters for those who ride the white-toothed glint

and if around the bend of each karst cliff
wind the wooden bridges into Shu
and you, noble in flight, betrayed by both kingdoms,
regard the splash beneath your horse's hooves,
suspended without fishing nets or spider
silk but a hidden thread nonetheless—then
who looks back at you from that moonlit surface,
serenely, with the force of non-seeing?
Lute-fluidic, my breast on hers, synovial sarcoma eating at her heels,
an overturned leaf searching for crickets on plum blossoms
as a sign of failed mandate—

    the hours are long waves asking

    why filiation chart?

    you fall and you rise and you fall to become

    the rest cannot be named

I cast my ink upon the white sea,
crowns and sons and silage and pox at the end of worry
arrowed ladies on swift horses   whose message nearly
saved the kingdom, dressed as a man

another desperate story will offset the context of my bladder.

True poverty is having no history
to spend its lost inheritance—
the celestial nun's betrothal
was to a goatherd who became Shen Neng, our first ancestor who
entered her astral hygiene and gave us moons
to cocoon our hopes—

written in the spring of 761.
Should we seal what we say with torte and
how long have you waited? How long
have you prolonged the five elsewheres, heart splayed against the hourglass,
while all that remains of you
is a gold hairpin,
and your secret needlework of lotus leaves?

meditation: 5 walls

It is the Japanese lilac's second flowering
out back where the lawn chair met last night's rain.
I hesitate before wiping off the drops—
these are delicate times, divining principles
derived from ear wax and meridians.
There are powers pulling me round the house
this morning, whose roofline
shades the grass and the tree shade on the grass
and the world is an enormous bowl of sense
collecting light and dark tadpoles.
Yin and yang
seem to speak for someone else;
or is it a figure of speech
passed on as the will to change?
Although the burning city leans its cut-out away from me
and the new day is only one more bomb away,
it's not enough. My blood's on the prowl
for another source. A tiny spider
on my wrist lifts its abdomen
positions its centre
and sails off into the thin parachute
of the air we call a nation.

the rabbit over Barbados

       look down:
space enough inside the eye

      for stars   and spare
           all seeing   rare

a tireless kingdom beggar waits to point the way that walks.. this colony turned paradise.. not creamless black spirits in the tensed calves that shimmer over sand.. he simply wants to hear the wild blue strain of things.. aged 13 nearly drowned his brain whispered.. so Weyman there's the green light above you.. so close but you can't get to it.. and your eyes windowpanes through a culture of muscled divers so at home on glint capped waves.. cirrus estrus.. hyle estrus.. my hearing underwater couldn't float.. Conway Twitty on the radio then the ukulele stylings of Israel Kamakawiwo'ole

     Old age   this   cat's cradle
           father and son pulling
    themselves
        inside out

he re-tooled his children

lu-thlu-pai

for screwdriver
    I handed
    him a hammer
    he swore and threw it down

beloved sea creature pull back your spines.. inside you just a tablespoon or two of brine..
urchin harvesting returns after 30 years trypanosome blue.. pink skirts of coral
Christo shipwrecked at Actium.. calm sandbars turn the gull away from magnetic north
while my mammal tits transmit like the spire of some local church who can't contain
Sunday.. on and on writs of daylight blessed non smiles.. I understand what the roaming..
blue gives.. optimism poured freely from a child's hand.. a second third fourth coming where
carbon dioxide dreams of ozone and I begin to write

what is not a book
has no cover only its own unsure lure
so how
can words be at the centre?

Wide-angled clutches
gardenias on the floor
pluperfect strands

I'd hand him his latest cigarettes from 7-Eleven

the dolphin's soft   plop shaped
then tail   switch
                                            glope

                                    Bussa In the Sky With Irons
and the cross chiasmic dubious messiness of the strands of life.. they bother and they worry
like retired gardeners on adirondacks.. gloves.. seeds.. arthritic nubs they are studying
weather.. how a cloud will branch along its edging nude sea creature with no instrument no
confusion.. belly tight water drops whose rearrangements sound like break and enter
                                                        ylang
                                                        ylang

                              One bright conscience sprung
                                      from a jolly jumper
                                      drooling city lamps on
                                      wide
                                      birthday cake

the closer I smell him
the more he builds himself an island
brick and cauldron. Stokes those backyard

    embers all night to boil the bamboo
    leafed *doong*. Inside,
    sticky rice fuses around each egg yolk
    and the *doong* bob up when done.

drops and drops falling.. wake up dear expectation.. sweet supine colon.. lay down islands
that censer grey day when heat was spooning up the equator and boiling over the higher
latitudes and good eating was about to change

Once my father told me
many times my father told me

how right it was
for the A-bomb to avenge Nanking

                    A taxi cab in Bridgetown turned over
                         they're hurt but laughing
                       and music so loud
              there's legend and provocation

window framed bilge of blue the life way up there.. cheesecake.. dried on one edge the
hotel's not interested.. how far the nation's plantation's edge Igbo Asante at Stroud Point
Yoruba Chandler Bay my eyes twitch closed even my pillow around both ears can't shut out
the keeled sand closes in.. begins to kneel this flat isle outward

after eating flying fish and breadfruit
I swam
a line so sweet
the Great Wall viewed from the moon said,

Innocence, bird or rain

                    you came
and your self-taught plummet
         sharpened me without the glint.

and newness.. rampant.. turned over leaf.. trumps constancy
half duplex on stilts eroded from St. Luke's Gully changed its stucco three times..
Crane Hotel overlooking the brochure of vistas eight sided turrets the spires and the servants
owing their sentence to each thing owed to its former colony.. laid down between

                    Air .. Sea

grooming the deep bent moon who only smiles down when you might bother looking up

                         Not enough
                         links
         the seashell and the monkey coil

         but mother tree spreads
                    her burled sorrows anyway

a spirit must be
separate from brain chemistry
                    said Kant
            who could
        water chlorophyll and panic

casting out immanence   as if
    enough were to simply observe
and then live our own life away from observation

                                        So

                                    I burrow through his eyes
            bridge the shanty   walk
                                    blue crabs on pink sand

a satchel of sea urchin
spiked across my shoulders

requiem

Always over me are jade dishes of rare meats, and the meaning of mercury around a funerary barge … such is my take on empire poetry, though even its tones in Cantonese tend to fall musically at the end.

A tone language could be sister to calligraphy where pitch and placement in the mind's air is key to the esthetic tension on the page—half-pictured equisyllables, idealogues of the valley and mountain stroke. Origami isn't far from this timely form, although the fix on sculpted interpolation is counterintuitive. Chinese poetry casts dreams as a foretaste of heaven. It likes impressionist waterlilies too, beds them down with forbearance and calm, and nymph shyness: *A maiden water-pure in the seclusion of grottoes.*

Reading this now seems dangerous and out of place. Hamas/Fatah gather. So do warm winters, and collapsed faiths. Goethe's worship of sorrow.

I sat with my sister conjuring spirits of the dead with a used birthday candle squashed in a meat pie tin. With closed eyes I recited the incantation. I could see the candle's synergic heat on my eyelids, our joined hands forming the horizon to a world that should open as easily as fairytales do. Then I thought I saw a ghost rolling its face out from the flame. The flame snuffed out, the circle broke, and we went running off screaming in all directions.

I'm starting to return to the wisdom of an eight-year-old, at least some of the time. Where nymphs can sun on our eyelids. Where gnosis and hiding can visit too.

4.

however brief

your toe cares to dip in

how could they forget my birthday?

Chinatown evening on frozen river camphor; toothpicks tag our lips.
Bellies full, we walk without talking.
Banker's Hall smoke stack a lavender holdover of the snuffed-out west.
There's no taking a back seat to old crimes, secret tunnels leading to escape ....

I ask him about it and he croons back, *Gong maht-ah-wah?*
which means, *Speaking what?*
What are you saying? although
the true inflection is more like,

tell me another story—
> Dad somewhere in the Wu Tang mountains
> asleep in the arms of another.

Chinese romance wrecks each dynasty with
fox maidens who open their lotus without
any forced parable. A life lived
away from observation. Betrothal ceremony somewhere in Hoi Seng:
you were 57 but not dead yet and
Step Mom finds some dried *pahk* leaves
in your suitcase after you get back. Your *Heng Ha*
home girl hanging off your beard that you sported for village-gossip,
and don't forget
that left pinky nail
you grew out emperor-like, for stabbing the cheek meat of sea bass.

As usual after an iron-clad rice meal, you're all wobbly root-Confucian,
sunny days by the handful, soy nuts and licorice.

politeness

I know this bird. A hundred years before Confucius, he perched.
Overheard Kuan Chang say, "A true prince makes the people his God."
His loopy nonsense, crossed with Karl Marx,
stretched out in august welcome
to this day. *Here and now,* said the bird of rays
in a mangosteen forest, weighing heavy on Dad's shoulders.
A juicy pangolin passed by,
claws folded in prayer. She declared,
"Animals do not become spirits after death.
Why should man alone succeed?"
Here and now, said the bird, perched not ten feet away
from the Emperor's soldiers.
Dad, just fourteen, approaches them
with a ball of opium in his skeletal hand
and a journey without direction.
Arigato.
The soldiers toss him a tin of food—sardines, probably.
Sika, they call him—small deer—his disappearance
through bamboo bracts loosens him.
Now he's all-out running and laughing
and crying—a gentleman's agreement
has saved him. Hands and mouth are sardine-dipped;
he knows he'll have to hunt here and now
above and beneath the indifferent
to feed his sister, his two brothers, his mother.
Hunting's the one bright thing in the world
lifting him like a balloon outside his tummy,
over the wall he faces before sleep.
Before waking.

b & w photo of Dad, 1954

2-toned spats, linked arm in arm gangster-style
with silver tie clips, blurred pant cuffs and

he's sneaking up the stairs to catch me dancing with myself
to my brother's 45 of *Draggin' the Line* by Tommy James

he's hot-blooded at 28, so good-looking on the street,
burning his jazz like an ulcer Chinese teens sipping malts
from dental-chromed lovelies, see he'd missed their scene by about a decade

A flash of telepathy, shame—I opened
my room door and found Dad crouched, giggling up
the stairs, though I knew what he in turn had listened to:
the drinking song from *Student Prince*, Garland's
*Get Happy, Barber Shop Chord, Who Stole
My Heart Away* (and *Greensleeves* too)

he kept these '45s locked away
dated '54 Chicago
where he stayed a year before Calgary, Chicago the photo,
him and all his buddies buzzed on motorstreetglare,
lefty-browed hatrims and
Chicago
unrolls its socks even if at Linda Mae's he chops up barbecue duck
for speedy service while his Marlboro matador cries *Toro*
to the cutest girls
munching on haw flakes and Sweet Maries.

a swallow's tail

for Fred Wah

Faces end conversation.
Eyelids lift and drop those who've fallen into the past.

Dad's partial plate shifts
while names fade from moon to home like a sleeve of light
reaching through cloud cover.

"Ahh, ahh, old Uncle Lu," he whispers.
Uncle Lu who befriended a large rat on the boat from China,
taught the rat to fetch like a dog, and if you touched his tail
he'd roll over.

Step Mom clears her throat at Dad's story, refutes it outright with something
about a Pekingese and a sweater, as she sheds her slippers and hovers off
to bed.
No more big fights that once exploded through the walls.
Her dentures are in the kitchen with Dad's, soaking in side-by-side teacups,
sort of a truce.
When Step Mom moved in, she put our first mother's fur coat
out with the trash, because ghosts still wear their clothing from time to time.
Wouldn't she have stroked the fur just once,
draped herself for a doubter's moment in its full warmth?
Not likely.
She was more scared of hauntings than of rats that roll over,
her frugal suits hand-made and sewn plainly
so as not to compete with the one who roams incense,
windows brightly in the halls.

I dream of my dead mother

Snow an essential furniture, falling
to the seven silk-stringed notes of a ch'in zither.
You're not bamboo-boned enough
for composition   leaves will autumn
                                        as the bailiff
Bombex fluffs out her wings. The end is as near as linen.

Years subtracted the vessel of its body—
a journey without deprivation wouldn't be enough.
Pilgrimage in 1989, we walked the summit of Mount T'ai,
7,000 steps up to the poets' stones,
their memorial shrine peeping
through paper, rock, and merchant stalls—
philosophers' words spared the country's call to arms in this mist.
You watched me watching you as snow fell,
each gondolier pushing
cold nothings between spiral arms, dust canals.
Summer's queen mother
has retired to grow tea-melons outside the green gate of Ch'ang-an,
pouring her infusion over morning clouds.
I checked the mail for quiet—
a sphinx without Egypt, a gong without ears.
No white dragon to ride, no rain,
no settle to the sighing roof.
Your face slept on the same earth
where I dug up gladiolus bulbs to winter them over.

Why are you still wiser than all my years without you?

Maybe a doorway opens from your hand to mine

                                        the way east

is where I wait for you in some quiet minus distance
where good rockets meet
names of places worn down to their vowels

patient study

1.

This green planet
wakes up; flinches, goes by
drouth to passover

lenient without
a master. Mice
slide out the tail-loose
ground.
          That was his dream—
the thrust of it.

Solstice in the grate,
what if?
rockets him to favour
with another race, but here
in the furry stupas
of diabetic hall with i.v. poles wed in red—
another silver flows in sheet music. Phalaenopsis and
          the best civet coffee
          "nothing new" say the sheep safely grazing
          mouths disappearing and spots as far as you can see
          Mom's voice that slammed down one more "good morning"
                    your Goya grin
                    shrivels imperceptibly

then she sees a line of urine down the Calvin and Hobbes of
his dwindled calf muscle
so did
pampering somehow
help? He feels
a filament in his groin,
apron strings
wrapped twice around to measure thinning.

Animal leash, friar-like
gown of breezes

is the only proof this side of your face while nakedness and blame
recoil us from pity,
noise, and sorcerer's oxides—
mercy and freedom can't be divided.

This morning he watched a man without legs
rinse his dentures in a cup.
Keats' few, sad, last grey hairs
seemed to worm in the dark have-nots
chin drawn in he recalls birdchirp from the birdclock
cardinal wren starling bitch
the twelve holy shapeshifts
feet over starless hills over Trout Lake then slumped in a wheelchair
from wheelchair to the next century
in the apse of St. Edmund's he heard a fart
it blew through like a declaration of
this body sweetened fork light from the eyes this
body
awash in roots of friends   ferment
parting the day just so
does this buttressed light
hold back windows
to hold back tears?

2.

It was the way
of being divided by zero
when I closed the door and struck up
the electron microscope's green-eyed beam.
Here, the weight of light mattered.

The tungsten filament spoored,
lit the font-intimate protein deposits
on capillary loops. Podocytes without
fenestration. Hindsight without experience.
On the stage of his epoxy-locked tissues
was a hidden book of names that didn't include mine;
his life was ending,
throwing diagrams on my wall while his flicker stalled.

If the real world is this city in the foothills,
and the stars are beyond our understanding, then
I think the stem that pushes thought and form out
in words and telomerases
is the compassionate life.

Chinook, Mu or Atlantean, hangs islands from its downhook.
Cloud up, horizon down, look for happy colours
if only they could be enough

look for the happy ones
as a feeding tube is for dirt
mere grains of sand aspiring
to be something that can outlast what's left from your figuring out
ear to earth's sternum
counting
then rephrasing the
long-leafed question:
why it
all ran out, got wasted, bled
you dry

3.

He recalls how nature and nowhere could be summoned.

His dad stuck an electric prod in the ground between the hollyhock and the asparagus bush. Soon worms writhed out of the ground. Dreams would recur every few years with the earth raised up and writhing worms engulfing him and pulling him deep down. His eyes opened wide and also writhed in this thickest blackest soil.

Heidegger said that the pilgrim already knows what it is he seeks.

4.

Rabbit returned one last time. He leaned not sadly
on a bagpipe, playing
someone's lung. Hearing its tired squeeze
in hospice, hissing
sunflowers, pushed daisies,
how to distinguish air from bone and bone from eternity
whose demarcation in the nerves must shunt privacy in the mind
away from hurt

"there's no justice or compassion on earth
without an emptying of the self"
Abdal Hakim Murad's paraphrase of a Sufi proverb

turn your fancy verbs to katyushas and those
bedevilled graces that gear your face towards effacement
I want no thank yous no favours just that
tick
that winces

5.

Something is not quite grasped
in the white crucible that switches words
and gold; just as limbs catch fire
to bypass the inner life. Good that
the limbs catch fire, just be careful
of the café spoon
that drops from worry
the homeless man pushing his legless sister out of hostel doors
to the downtown park where he stands over her wheelchair
ransoming her plight against his own
the mirror frame I look through
sorting animalcules from aircastles
the ashes he smoked
cigarette end bounced off a rock in Bora Bora
I believed curtains would part the one condition empathy affords
and the terms I inherit

5.

think too hard

& you lose strength

the terrorist at O'Hare airport

A red sunrise over Chicago. Its rice paddy soothes me.
It gazes through shoji at five thousand years'
bending over.

The Great Frost was not unlike Orlando's sleep, numb flip-side of what
Emily Carr called joy and movement, her last paintings
spent amplifying tree-sense.
Spent shoreline. Emptiness. Suicide
in a deep blue palette.

Calm has always been what desire wants. What it can't have.
I have only now faced the end, sipping tea.
Mom died with her eyes on.
A field frocked in Lady Lipstick—
my daughter's name for wild summer paintbrush.

The towers never fell for just one person.
At Gate 11, an East Indian woman woke me,
asked if I needed anything at Starbucks; she needed coffee *now*.
I blurted out, "No thanks; I'll watch your luggage."
Right away June said, "You can't watch other peoples' luggage!"
"Smart girl!" the woman answered back.

She tried again, asking an old man if he needed anything at the Starbucks.
He obliged with an easy nod.

The woman's luggage sat for half an hour between him and I.
During that time, I began to imagine ticking sounds emanating
from her Tourister. I let Stephanie climb on my lap, all the while
imagining the explosion, the faces strewn on contact with a miniature sun—
June and I and our beautiful daughters bombed out of this moment—gone.

Could this happen?
I looked at Janine, reading *Trumpet of the Swan*,
and Stephanie, making bug-eyed dragons out of our hands.

It seemed enough, suddenly, to be surrounded by a fuzzy cuteness
that came from the insides of our children. Better yet,
what proceeded from that
was everyone's recognition of life,
the genuine amazement of it,
which could only be torn down and rebuilt in a child's face.

The good news is
I am nearly asleep on the airplane with my family around me.
The East Indian lady has gone barefoot, stretching her dark-painted toenails
into the aisle as she angles with her nine bracelets for a pillow
and conversation.

cookie's fortune

I want memory to teach me
more than a speeding plane window—
us fleeing Hurricane Jeanne out of Orlando, and
you pointing at a set of shoes in *Sky Mall* magazine
and ignoring the Doctor Without Borders
mapping out an eye defect on a napkin:
river blindness caused by worms in the bloodstream.

You showed me these ingenious shoes with
long nails in the soles,
meant for aerating the lawn as the wearer (you're
presuming me, for whatever reason), stomped across his yard, back
and forth over the same turf, for years.

It's true. Time to think about home and yard again,
after Epcot's sugar-coated pavilions and Eiffel mock-up.
The happiest place on earth cut short by atmospheric threats.

So I drifted off
holding your hand
that became the fortune cookie
Dad gave me as he started to cut my hair.
I screamed as one wrong snip
drew blood from my ear and Mom was there
holding me—
the very weight of hurt
lifted away and pulled close to her heart.
Is that what love is?
No stiff upper lip required.
Just an easy up,
and quick transport towards voices in the other room.

monday thaw

On TV it looked like a high-speed photo of a milk drop,
the dying leader of the Pana Wave laboratory cult smack in the
centre.
Acres of white cloth streamered his followers, who
circled him like crown jewels.

More and more I'm responding to stark white on black,
letting the morning frost finish for me.

Calgary is fur-lined in the sun. Although the cold front
will chop us down to minus, there are hints of a melt.
Dad's three-legged shadow bends blueness
on the salt grained snow.
His cane stabs seed grasses that hang in dead doublets over a pond.
No goddess-catching here on the sly, icy bends of Bowness Park.

We trudge over a footbridge, just as a skater passes under us.
And though he calls his legs *moi-yoong*, good-for-nothing,
it's still the best uncertainty that finds us here.
Beneath the white ice, light is reaching down
and allowing self-assemblage—
strong wind with minimum repose
for dragons about to wake.
Skin is ever folding inward, shaping new drives
that rise from nothing,
into the same white hourglass.

We start over again
by inversion.
Snow pours down from one bell to the other.

spaceships

On a tall evening, 1969, just after Christmas,
my brother and I are looking out of our brand new toy binoculars,
out of our toy binoculars into the wide night sky.
It's a dark, high-window night

pressed down on my face: even more intensified by the
warm pajamas against my skin, and my brother and I at peace
on his bed, and my two sisters in their cots
writing their names on the living room wall with new flashlights.

Absurd to say this nearly forty years later—
but I never felt so at home in my life as I did then
with my brother, surrounded by the clearness of being here
and a question I wanted to ask of it,
one I felt I might someday know the answer to

if only I dreamed a little harder.
Across the street were the two highest trees in the entire neighbourhood:
Ms. Baker's wild aspens.
They took up half her front yard, shading her lime-trimmed home
all year round. Tonight,
flitting like a giant firefly behind those branches,
was the U.F.O. My brother explained what that stood for.

Through the plastic lenses of our binoculars you couldn't even see
its hovering xenon disc—
just a bright-spinning z,
one edge blue, the other, orange.
My mind shot forward to a future, a clearly imagined future,
where I found myself on a planet accustomed
to the comings and goings of spaceships.
Aliens on the streets; in the schools; dining with us.

So I kept my own counsel, pitched my surprise
to match my brother's, as he kept saying,
"What the heck is that?"

And when my sisters crowded beside us
to look up at the visitors from far away,
we all wondered if we were the only ones watching them.

It was then that I realized
that the aliens were at least as curious as we were,
only looking down at us from their spaceship windows
but not only looking down at us. They were deciding
on which snowy roof to land.

"Pick ours," I whispered under my breath. "Pick ours."

beauty thread

Two mothers—one living, one dead.
I keep thinking it's sensible
to obey one while searching for the other.

Imagine all the watered garden vegetables,
all the plucked and rinsed spinach leaves
hiding our first mother's eyelids:

when you took our faces into your
dish pan hands, your cracked affections
falling from the title, "Step mother"—

did you for even a second pretend
that we could be your children, too?
In the early days you really did try:

you opened a maple cabinet
revealing to us a box of fine white powder.
You dusted my sister's face then fashioned a triangle
of sewing thread between your thumbs and index fingers.
The triangle opened and closed

like a scissor, the thread spun as it hovered
over my sister's peach-fuzzed upper lip
and chin. The spinning thread

twisted as it tore off and gathered up
the translucent hairs of my sister's face.
Her eyes watered but somehow

she held her neck motionless.
Her eyes sank into reverence
for you, our Step Mom, whose steady thread

would reap the days from our giving,
and you would
find us too much work, too much

a reminder of what a slave you were
to children that weren't truly grateful or
biologically yours.

But for now, because
no one has cared for my sister like this
since our Mom died four years ago,

your thread is a loom
for the curtain of beauty
that my sister passes through.

not an aphid

No flower of my blood,
the good senior citizen in the mall
heard the earth whispering. She heard it not long after
spilling a soft drink down her wooden leg
which had to be removed
so that its cup wouldn't run over
and soak the fleshy nub of her knee.

Rushing in from soft cowls along the riverbed and
colours swinging past my eyes,
I propped her up on one side,
smelled her purse and underthings
that start out small and end
as monster bushes by summer's end.
Their song is elsewhere, as prosthetics
and etiquette admonish us to bend dutifully
to the bent crocus head and lift
up its damaged ends as
if they were our own.

I saw her artificial leg
and its Pepsi-soaked stocking bounce
on the floor like a snapped lotus.
Earth whispered
inside her leaf, my bloodstream,
bundles of mitochondria, stacks of chloroplast—
we stirred some kind of cauldron together,
her and I, at least the same
embarrassment that took its cue
from the story of an ant milking
the serum of aphids.

Whether or not I listened
well enough to life that
only needs to rise
and serve with no complaint, I'll never know,
although she, the elderly woman,
was by no means an aphid. She had both
art and aesthetics on her side
as she hit me over the head with it
when I tried to
put her back together again.

somewhat of an apology

1.

Someone theorized we were more energy than being.
If we were small enough and just massless enough to
let go of the weight in us that induces gravity,
we'd be flitting two places at once at the speed of light.

Mrs. Tachibana
thoroughly and nectarly folds silver paper triangles,
building them with her good hand into a crane sunning on one foot.
It fits my hand like a small echo chamber
        a scrolling Arabic
                or a wing

I've only met her once to ask her
what it was like at 8:15 in the morning of August 6
when the sun came down to play.
Having touched glory

you see in her half-melted hand all the faith and strength imparted by a B-29,
the years of operations and re-training
to become a beautician in New York City
bold silky smiles, pin-curled perms and salon Dior honey ripples—
to have all that space given
back from nightmare   arm
bent upwards with its ragskin leaves
that darken
and connect a burning land to falling signs and

points of worry that keep the wheel busy and so very loud

every year has been lived in the middle of the road.
Children intersect lines of geese returning
to Calgary for the peace march

                              memory into memory
even birds' eyes can overshoot the wetland

as if feeling over seeing is the deeper calling here
and beauty can be allegory too
                              for the quiet
warming your once burnt
but now consolable hand
fashioned from lightness
now busily attending

2.

At the Sakura tea party, she wears a blue kimono with cornflowers. Surging
grass.

There are always 5 answers to the 5 elements.
Pulse-taking is an art
so use ascending method to dispel *chi* stagnation. This promotes defecation,
say the experts.
Through moxibustion and faith in my own liver, I've moved away
from middle *jiao*. My *chi* has dispersed,
my pulse is scattered. Serotonin will not cross
the white colt bridge tonight.

I thought I could be the leaf that lufts upwards
whose early red is the wavelength closest to visible heat
before the sun's glare mellows it
which as a child I used to think was strange
that no one alive could face the sun eye to eye
so I began to write a beginning
where everyone's eyes were made of crystal
and vision couldn't be burned out of you. The story
needed the kind of hero that's required in today's market.

I didn't understand then
what the world demanded of a hero. I was only following
the slippery slope of lassitude
by doing nothing.
I think I'd prefer to cast
the first stone and then run like hell.

3.

Kafka invented the safety helmet out of concern for all the injury claims he
dealt with as a lawyer for an Austrian insurance company. Kafka read each
claim out loud, to feel every bone-crushing detail. He had to, otherwise the
perfect pain of expression would be purely decorative and purposeless. Maybe
he already (hacking his lungs out) foresaw this aspect: how the soft and
visceral appurtenances of feeling are too soon diminished, having been
mangled and torn from the original experience. All that's left is the apron
string after being led from childhood into this daily grey soupishness—with no
further unexpected deviations from torment. Injury is the wild card, which
ensures torment, which ensures the hand of God. As much as Kafka helped to
prevent deaths, I'd also like to think that he revelled in certain cases of
unforeseeable tragedy. This served to broaden his theme of helplessness,
where healing is not preferred, and words of comfort ring out like bad
commentary.

4.

I've outlived those consumptive artists from the last two centuries,
most of whom died before 40.
Stranded by name and page number on weary lakes

drinking grasses out of the ground
lives avowed and thwarted
and pulsed after with societal upheaval and porn-like star-wipes.
It's enough to want to become chaste

given these blogs and shit and drivel.
Prototypical death-poem diaries only serve to milk the
will to live.
I've seen this before
over thatched roofs, ponds that change their tune,
flash cinders, blow away sweetness and turn their skeleton over in the soil.
Many wishes fail, attract worms,
and still fail. I envy the crickets who come out when children play.

5.

Supposing that the weight of night over us
is a natural process, and that sleep and gravity are fluids
that can be sweated out of our bodies,
then the night will have to be accounted for in its fullest dimension.
More importantly, we will have to account for the guilt-rest,
the limp clocks that power our optimism.
Without sleep, without gravity, we
can better slip into our natural moons and see ourselves
rubbing noses with the two-faced goddess of Autumn and Spring.

The world away is the vampire world. It's the one that draws us up
like that one-celled animal who must taste first
through jellied tentacles. Its arms absorb me,
like the Blob's metabolic suffocation
that subsumes vitals
and servo-mercurial vapours.
Gobbled up in one day
in such a seemingly uncaring way, I can only
conclude that the enterprise
is full of cosmic intentions. Therefore
it cannot lack deliberateness and caring.
You can almost call it bittersweet.

6.

I don't know what this noise is
through the swarm:
an overhead forest should be named by its grouping
of winds;
its branching pupil underneath and above me
who floats in the middle of its eye.
We're so much inside each other
that it compels me as much through unconscious radiance as it would
through some profound translation:

a toy blue piano plink

a soft bedroom whisper saying, *Oh, veiled one …*

my obliques and deltoids surround the heartbeat that slips off,
while gleam returns to every apple tree.
If temptation can be crossed through willed senses
and words that distinguish the connection from the countenance,
then I think skin,
our most common adjective,
will be ready to make the leap.
It would be a lot like the fisherman who returns a fish to the stream.
Why not?
We don't know anyone else except ourselves.
Our dreams were created so we could take what's forbidden
without doing real harm.
A bomb dropped over half a century ago
can finally submit to a gentler radiation
thrown out from our hands
that reach down and see the
fortunate folds that go on to re-shape
and imitate art that's not deluded
by inexperience,
or fooled through old attachments.

meditation: 6 walls

Once upon a time, monastic nomads ....
No. I wanted to close my eyes
beside June and begin
on bended knee, the lover's midnight tangent, but
like the zero which monks a space
you never thought of,
I'm swirling tonight beneath our covers.
I begin to follow
an old pathway dreamed around a circular garden.

Buddha and St. Peter are saying modest hellos
as they pass us by on floating feet.
Everyone is turning away from the everlasting,
back to my dad's back yard
with that cauldron of sticky rice dumplings
boiled in bamboo leaves.
Meanwhile, the wind is throwing down
the sun's leaflets, as if to surrender some
easy ransom. This happens
so casually

that the noise from the laundry room
also funnels into my brain—
the tumbling running shoe
that kicks open the dryer door at midnight
becomes the pearly gate that rolls off its hinges,
letting everyone come and go as they please.

6.

and Yi the Archer shot nine suns

only one his bowstring spared

at work

1.

Man on a crash cart, moaning
as the elevator shuts.
Paramedics restrain him. Man sneezes so hard
his nose breaks.
No, just a coil of white fleshy
round worm. It curls
once about his philtrum and lip,
and falls asleep.

2.

Patient, shaved-head electrodes,
his powder-blue gown open at the spine,
shows off his intelligence, says,
"Don't worry, Ma. I'm fine. The yoga helps."
I see a Zen koan in the sagged skin above his ass. A cross
or leash around his neck pulls him ....

"Shooters!"
he waves at me, his face suddenly animated. He's pointing
to the beaker in my hand.
"No," I tell him. "Urine."

3.

Keats' "few, sad, last grey hairs"
on an old man's head. They say that one hair is left on the shaven crown
of a dying Moslem, so that Mohammed can draw him up to heaven.
They say that mandrake root pulled from earth, cries out.
At midnight, my fever spikes.
I close my eyes and leave. Return

small and confused
by these prostrations, intimations
of life's detachment, though you can't trust any higher institution
that debits mercy, credits despair.

4.

Next day at work, I close myself into darkness. Press the button that flows
75 thousand volts into a tungsten filament, stripping electrons from its
surface. At ten thousand magnifications, I look for Herpes virus.
Cytomegalovirus. Rule out Candida.

Icosahedral, spherical or filamentous, they re-write our cells in a field of green
light. Illness crystallized. Short wavelengths of electron light allow me to see
what visual light can't. I used to think that the day-to-day perceptions seen
through flesh and veins were experiential. But the truth is, we're like dragons
thrown as shadows on the wall.

The real world is smaller than we are. A Chinese lantern emanates my thoughts
and form outward, until I catch myself blurred and magnified, as diffuse as
consciousness bending myths around a lit life.

"Home sweet home," she whispers, wheeled into Palliative Care, her chart
binder tucked behind her knees. In her voice, cold dead leverage of pneumonia.

5.

Small, happy
hanging habeneras
on the sill at home in half-light
do not need surgery after they're picked.

They are reminding me of what shouldn't
be eaten after midnight, primal as a cut finger

but also whispering like thin Buddhas:
transcend, anastamose this desire to have
with the desire to have not. This is
common knowledge
with any bell pepper at midnight.

6.

Systems beyond our control—
lady walks in pregnant;
rolls out emptied and rid of it.
My reason for watching is, to protect a way of healing
crouched in metaphor—needle pokes, test tubes, touch-and-go
respirations that efface the smiling bedpan. It
slid beautifully over the caul of it,
skin over skin hemmed in
and petrified.
Knife in; knife out.
Our angel of measurements.

7.

Small. Indispensable. Shady half-lives.
Cancers flare and retreat. Candles come and go
and no one hears the flame snuff out.
It's the orderly, ordinary hush of hearing
each expanse in breath and wondering who
put cells in there to cradle-catch the air.

Why atmosphere pushes down
to hypnotize the runner with exhaustion. This
body   this sometimes falcon-like
fall from recovery and then to believe

with all the science of your heart
that all we have is this body: to believe
that lightning and storms, dart frogs and excoriations
that bend leaves at night, and our children,
our progeny of longing, are born from and follow
the footprint of all we have: this body

8.

Skeletons and systems are like the moon without her rabbit—
almost featureless, almost rising into plain feature.

Jazz clouds play lightly across its pinkeye,
forest fire up north, I guess. It's been a dry October,
5 years exactly since June's mother died. Her gravid
white eyes in a bruised face, I've nearly forgotten.

There are no more alchemies. No elixirs
to outlive this going.
I touch June's hand and know I belong to her. We forget
how cold air spreads our breaths into uncertainty
and when we speak, this warm intent is forked
by the tongue into words,
half-truths that bypass the inner life.
Just the limbs catch fire:
be careful of your heart. Even a good heart
can throw a clot, unleash emboli
like time's arrow

9.

Productive criteria, says Dr. Graves. His sister-in-law's
daughters were carrying fresh persimmons when the bombs fell on Iraq.

"Epidemiology relies on productive criteria."
The science of sickness spreading, pandemics and such
requires exactitude. Violin-fingers.
Superimposed on Dr. Graves' tall body is the accident
of being American and the accident of a world
getting too small for common sense.
Accidental meetings in the dark-hearted forests of Africa.
It's an old doomsday story, despite the beautiful day,
beautiful clouds outside. The sky is *us* out there.
Why am I talking to Dr. Graves?
Maybe I want to re-live my own usefulness.
"Am I moral?" is the first question that pops up.
I was under cover of hedges. Ambushed that pro-Nazi
kid just in front of the candy store. Hit him in the face
for not believing how many Jews died. Right in front
of Mr. Ergang's candy store. Mr. Ergang had been with the Hitler Youth,
age 16, saluting the Fuhrer himself. Mr. Ergang
came out of the store, laughing. Put his hands on both our shoulders
and led us into his store for free Hershey's Kisses.

10.

Protect everyone if you can. Protect only yourself if you can.
At work, another elevator ride. Another dying, diabetic smile.

Eschatology is dead. She circles the sun and the sun
circles our body of touch, thrust, memory, grace.

Old dialectics like good and evil
stay with me. Nowhere to go but here

between the whites of my own eyes—
arc of *us* blading through winter into spring.

And the wait for nothing
comes and glows

when I look for, then find at the edge of my sight, Pleiades.
I know it's Pleiades by how it appears and disappears

through the retina's blind spot: dark heaven
gives symmetry to our faith.

Histology

1.

Before the anvil at dawn, between
the cloud's fiction and the world's end,
there appeared to me an old man
I knew I could be.
Sadness swung in his background. There were
arrowheads of forgotten hordes, a smell of horse,
and skeptical perfection
which pulled at his face like
one whose brain was crystallized with the same
amyloid plaques that freshen spider silk.
The day called him out to play.

He told me about Wei Sheng who, centuries before Christ,
waited for his love beneath a bridge pillar, composed
poetry on rice paper even as he drowned
from rising waters.
Afterwards the lasting tribute to love: myriad candle-lanterns set afloat,
Tai horsemen with white flags on shore, Yu-Chung hills
arrowed with swallows. The river
blossomed with flowers and pilgrims at night,
cloud-swallowed heaven ducking its approval, no, yes?
The old man kept looking up as he rubbed his hands
over an invisible fire.
He saw clouds overhead as he saw life—
silver lining in need of effacement, word-pearled
oxygens preparing for constant autumn
which, in awe of itself, became a wedded monk.

"I'm spoken for," he said,
"and I've blown the cliché that enough is enough for any one of us
caught between dragons and beggars
and the drowning politick of a heavy hand—
we who were taught to believe in

sins, wonders, signs,
all in the name of seven."

2.

In Calgary, as in Jinan,
I'm pissing away the half month
that coincides with plague. Everyone's piss
expects this: Rabbit has gone fishing.
I forgot how autumn ruled the neurotic,
bureaucratic crap of larkspur and meadow rue,
twigs kicking, a bamboo sea inside my breath,
this lab tech at work who, four months after Tiananmen,
drove to Vancouver, shipped out and joined the Students' Movement.
She wanted to fight for something,
rise up against (this
before iPods and nano-links)
secretaries of interior fiddlers—

but the poor keep falling through.
Should the ice of Calgary be white enough for the festive air,
where shit only smells clean
when there's nothing else to breathe?
What about the first buds along the river? No,
they're just last year's red clung rosehips,
hard done by, but ever-faithful—
                    a fairyland refers to a fairy story.

China of hemp gorse and hawthorn:
        I'm no good sacrifice
        for you.

And in the frozen morning cure-all, the old man
visited me one last time and left me between rib spreaders on the cutting table.

"My brush once defied the shape of things,"
he pined, rising from the chair, paper in hand, inkstone
and brush clattering. With tired
red eyes, he showed me the window, pointed up at the
stars, and I somehow knew their names—
Southern Palace, Jade String, Well-rope.

None of them shone in my name.

I thought that he'd leave his
last orders by my side, that the scroll of wisdom
was mine to keep: but I was wrong
and anyhow, the old
man's fragile distance was too genuine
and familiar to me. Like a father's.

I passively turned away.

"Although you feel nothing," he said,
tipping his hat goodbye,
"you are an insurrection against nothingness."

What did he mean by that?

I saw my tissues wrapped in lens paper, dunked in formalin baths,
nun of the processor slicing me down to handrails,
laces dangled, my bowtie drool-stained as proof
of the hand behind the walking stick,
doddering on and on
towards the footprint
of an older god.

Why older?
Older is as older gets—to believe in a slower, lasting
knife of our outward forms, while

the wounded generation, at peace
with its rage after ages of war, retires to
its bed—let someone else call a drill,
a gong to sound retreat,
a drum to sound attack:
clear a path
between fly-sense and innocence,
mini-guts on a windowsill
shined up like tubes in an old ham radio—

the time for insulin
is now. My writing
pees the city pure

for (my eyes give up)
those long thin canals of Jinan in '89
where a Mao-dressed woman with twenty foot pole
pushed her freight barge just under a moon bridge.
Leaping prow to stern, either side cleared barely an inch,
she blazed younger, more raven. She sailed
down the starry river,
burned past terra cotta into Shang bronze,
and slipped underground. Night soil
wears an unassuming gate,
as if we could merely be
these beautiful bags of breath after we go,
a sleepy fume
separate from this carry-on business.

But the buds leap and they crawl
from dead roots. They play peek-a-boo
with constant autumn
and elder cold fronts bawling from the heat,
baby's breath and cathedral bells that preserve return
every time the sun sets.

Suspended from the ceiling—
a night globe wrapped in rice paper.

There once was an old man
who I knew I could be.
Now he spreads his nights
farting and pushing obsolete star charts
off my table.

7.

neither here

nor

noise

1.

before the long walk outward to being born

a star lit through   with no doubt but that of its travels
down the grass heights that know
nothing of the will of wheels and drinking vessels

there was only the tome of light like two coins clanging in the air
that high deep silver pitch where Dad
struck two quarters together that showered me with my own hearing
one was silver
                    keeeeeeeeeeennnnn
                                        its song was like one world
among many in formation and any amount of tarnish didn't matter.
That sound knew how to fill me through and through.

The red gong bears horses
outward by the neck   we hear it and yoke
        powers invested
    to stay or laugh or be vigilant against terror

of the drum or cymbal that sees me
stranded and deranged by liberation
        and only through music
        did I get a sense of that lack or by some
    interplay or connection I became that

solvent current long lasting but never free

carried outward as if born to it

2.

so maybe laughter speaks of a presence
that's outside the body   uncontained
but once contained   it shapes the random asteroid circling above your tent

what are the chances?
its suspended sentence

listen to the question
the butterfly tastes through its feet
and sees fit to dream
with fire comes the delight of fire
and the fullest being must eventually answer to its own will
so free will
shouldn't dread what murders it
                    and nothing's sacred
                    if you aren't
                    new to you
                    and somehow revered inside

                                        it's said that you should loosen your tunic
                                        when the journey turns you homeward

so the only effective happenstance

                                        when the owl hoot
                                        calls the dead away

is hope for continuance
every nerve has a different scream
the scared and the attached
of which nothing's granted or foreseen
all things being equal take their outward forms or leave them
crying out   a night

that speaks for all of us

pauses.
Its name
goes into the cold fixed distance
and your path changes

3.

permanence likes to read where we came from
spirit without permanence feeds
on hesitation
giving us the grand old theme

the hard external casing that liquefies my verb
serving the infant
as I try to move towards the visible gestation of a star leaving the
underside of some heavenly body
with such solid love for unsolid things

all that's left to join substance with shadow
is the art of reading

how do I even gesture without it seeming forced
if seduction and entrapment of a word can't
bear the loudness of any one personality
so if time can be noted and poured out
as a continuous standing vase

then this must surely be the place where another stem without movement
transmits its anxiety
where the spirit that you exit or inhabit
merely laughs at the notion of birth or death
such reversals don't mean anything any more
nothing was rushed   nothing took its time
nothing was found or abandoned
and the ink and the water never loved one another

they were just there lazing
        on voluntary sunbeams

4.

so the referential

pose
juxta

every surface
bells perception's palsy
custodial as *we* seems
to converge
self
folded into
that which
can escape

or maybe you're
in one of your moods
telling
collectives to disperse
find your own ball
chasing the
phasic
mind body aphasia

soiled
the master narrative
deaf as dragons
is *ngee loong*
in Toi San

5.

now the post colonial genie is a language bomb
explode to detonate

ontologies and empyrean pantheons
will bear the law
if Heaven
bears the rest

hackers like Prometheus and Monkey King

metabolize master slave inner
outer tongue are they
specific enough for what polemic critical populist amoral
what in the world was I

when partisan rhetoric
represented a kind of clearing I
needed to claim at the end of my blot

fast bus cutting through the forest from Malacca to Kuala Lampur.
Thank God for the air conditioned view of rubber trees
palms square nets tipped at their Dutch centres down towards
the shore water   bamboo stilted shacks
set in the low angled wand of the sun.
Our bus knew the shapeshifting
blackblue sky flitting on reflective windows. I'm
ossified by this forest
that pluralizes history/flight

the big
uneasy

Mom still yanks me into her arms
away from his scissors.
Her fidelity
becomes my stance.

Some days it wears like a bad haircut
but it's a stance I live for nonetheless.

where it ends

so he was saying on TV that his left leg
felt foreign he needed
to cut it off   a fifty year desire ever since
he was a child   it's not me   me ends right here
above the knee
this line's ferocious
angry with warning like a hole
in the ground where the wasps are starting to hive

a funnelled buzz that gets too loud except
for the roar   its crystal amnesia
finds him shouting no matter what anyone says about the
mute weight   killing him
if only a mountain could appreciate the crazed distance with which he sees
himself

and then his wife helps him ease his leg into a tub of dry ice
does his line become an ulterior motive
holiday for the skin to be free
of the permission surrounding its senses
while the compass argues north

and his wife's love
ambient as formless weather rearranges
the phantom he glides on
out of sight   out of mind

evening is a verb

There's an intuitive side
to the leaf that darkens.
It flicks your eyelash before you know
that you've blinked.
A one-time shard
that seemed like rain yesterday. A child's
button that hangs like an unused question mark.
There's understood hype
that tomorrow will find better use for today's talents.

Maybe that's why I've let myself
follow the clues that safety and predictability leave.
In the past I've been leery of the mind's words.
Although they'd burn like maidens
and then dry me up again,
I knew they were
the sweetest choice I had for exploring need,
making good on my body lying in wait for its desire.
I'd return and be pinned to her legs like
two shining candles
solitary and anywhere at the same time.
Behind what you can't marry is
the other life that grows bit by bit,
pushing out your heart in tree-rings.
Fabulous was put on earth
to hear this bloodrush. You speak,
and the world reels. And no one will read
you better than yourself. No one will pull out
from under you this area of peace
you've made by artistry
and small cares built up
from the core. No one can say
how well you lived or how long it lasted,
this need to expect growth
and then be burdened by it.

Acknowledgements

This book is dedicated to June and Janine and Stephanie. In memory of Dr. Charles Steele. Dad's ever-presence. In memory of Wai Kuen Chan. The abiding grace of Mom, and my beloved sisters and brother.

Thanks to Sharron Proulx and the Wordweavers Writing Collective, Sarah Murphy, Vivian Hansen, Stuart McKay, Richard Harrison, Christopher Wiseman, Rita Wong.

To Misako Tachibana, a survivor of Hiroshima, who told me her story.

Without a generous writing grant from the Alberta Foundation for the Arts, this book would not be what it is today.

Sources

Zen and the Sutras, Albert Low, Tuttle Publishing/Raincoast Books, 2000.
Chinese Fairy Tales & Fantasies, Moss Roberts, trans./ed., Pantheon Books, 1979.
Folktales of China, Wolfram Eberhard, ed., Washington Square Press, 1973.
Chuang-tzu, the Inner Chapters, A. C. Graham, Unwin Paperbacks, 1989.
The Gossamer Years: The Diary of a Noblewoman of Heian Japan, Michitsuna no Haha, Edward Seidensticker, tr., Charles E. Tuttle Company, 1964.

Some of these poems were previously read on CBC *Alberta Anthology*, or published in an earlier form in the following literary magazines: *The Capilano Review*, *Westcoastline*, *filling Station*, *Arc*, *dANDelion*, *Alberta Views*. Thanks to the editors